First World War
and Army of Occupation
War Diary
France, Belgium and Germany

2 DIVISION
5 Infantry Brigade
Royal Inniskilling Fusiliers
2nd Battalion
1 January 1915 - 31 December 1915

WO95/1350/1

The Naval & Military Press Ltd
www.nmarchive.com
Published in association with The National Archives

Published by

The Naval & Military Press Ltd

Unit 10 Ridgewood Industrial Park,

Uckfield, East Sussex,

TN22 5QE England

Tel: +44 (0) 1825 749494

www.naval-military-press.com

www.nmarchive.com

This diary has been reprinted in facsimile from the original. Any imperfections are inevitably reproduced and the quality may fall short of modern type and cartographic standards.

© **Crown Copyright**
Images reproduced by permission of The National Archives, London, England, 2015.

Contents

Document type	Place/Title	Date From	Date To
Heading	2nd Division 5th Infy Bde 2nd Battalion Royal Inniskilling Fusiliers 1915 Jan-1915 Dec		
Heading	War Diary 2nd Battn. The Royal Inniskilling Fusiliers. January 1915		
War Diary	Wisques	01/01/1915	24/01/1915
War Diary	Wittes	25/01/1915	25/01/1915
War Diary	Robecq	26/01/1915	29/01/1915
War Diary	Les Choquaux	30/01/1915	31/01/1915
Heading	War Diary 2nd Battn. The Royal Inniskilling Fusiliers. February 1915		
War Diary	Les Choquaux	01/02/1915	05/02/1915
War Diary	Festubert	06/02/1915	06/02/1915
War Diary	Le Plantin	06/02/1915	12/02/1915
War Diary	Festubert	13/02/1915	13/02/1915
War Diary	Le Plantin	13/02/1915	14/02/1915
War Diary	Essars	15/02/1915	17/02/1915
War Diary	Gorre	18/02/1915	21/02/1915
War Diary	Festubert	22/02/1915	22/02/1915
War Diary	Le Plantin	23/02/1915	24/02/1915
War Diary	Bethune	25/02/1915	27/02/1915
War Diary	Cuinchy	28/02/1915	28/02/1915
Heading	War Diary 2nd Battn. The Royal Inniskilling Fusiliers. March 1915		
War Diary	Cuinchy	01/03/1915	03/03/1915
War Diary	Beuvry	04/03/1915	07/03/1915
War Diary	Cuinchy	08/03/1915	11/03/1915
War Diary	Beuvry	12/03/1915	15/03/1915
War Diary	Cuinchy	16/03/1915	19/03/1915
War Diary	Beuvry	20/03/1915	20/03/1915
War Diary	Vendin	21/03/1915	21/03/1915
War Diary	Gorre	22/03/1915	27/03/1915
War Diary	Festubert	28/03/1915	31/03/1915
Heading	War Diary 2nd Battn. The Royal Inniskilling Fusiliers. April 1915		
War Diary	Festubert	01/04/1915	04/04/1915
War Diary	Essars	05/04/1915	12/04/1915
War Diary	Festubert	13/04/1915	19/04/1915
War Diary	Bethune	20/04/1915	30/04/1915
Heading	War Diary 2nd Battn. The Royal Inniskilling Fusiliers May 1915		
War Diary		01/05/1915	31/05/1915
Heading	War Diary 2nd Battn. The Royal Inniskilling Fusiliers. July 1915		
War Diary		01/07/1915	31/07/1915
Heading	War Diary 2nd Battn. The Royal Inniskilling Fusiliers. June 1915		
War Diary		01/06/1915	30/06/1915
Heading	2nd Royal Inniskilling Fus Vol XIII From 1-31.8.15		
War Diary		01/08/1915	31/08/1915
Heading	2nd Royal Inniskilling Fus Sept 15		

War Diary	Bertrancourt	01/09/1915	30/09/1915
Heading	2nd Inniskilling Fus Vol XV Oct 15		
War Diary	Bertrancourt	01/10/1915	31/10/1915
Heading	5th Division 14th Bde 2nd Royal Inniskilling Fus November 1915 Came From G.H.Q. Troops 18 Nov 1915		
Heading	Came from G.H.Q. Troops 18th Nov. 1915 2nd R. Inniskilling Fusiliers November 1915		
War Diary		01/11/1915	30/11/1915
Miscellaneous	C Form (Original). Messages And Signals.		
Miscellaneous	C Form (Triplicate). Messages And Signals.		
Miscellaneous	Intelligence Officers Report to 4pm 2nd R. Inniskilling Fusiliers	22/11/1915	22/11/1915
Miscellaneous	Intelligence Officers Report to 4pm 2nd Royal Inniskilling Fusiliers	23/11/1915	23/11/1915
Miscellaneous	2nd Royal Inniskilling Fusiliers Intelligence Officers Report	24/11/1915	24/11/1915
Miscellaneous	2nd Royal Inniskilling Fusiliers Intelligence Officers Report	25/11/1915	25/11/1915
Miscellaneous	2nd Royal Inniskilling Fusiliers Intelligence Officers Report	26/11/1915	26/11/1915
Miscellaneous	2nd Royal Inniskilling Fusiliers Intelligence Officers Report	28/11/1915	28/11/1915
Miscellaneous	2nd Royal Inniskilling Fusiliers Intelligence Officers Report	27/11/1915	27/11/1915
Miscellaneous	2nd Royal Inniskilling Fusiliers Intelligence Officers Report	29/11/1915	29/11/1915
Miscellaneous	2nd Royal Inniskilling Fusiliers Intelligence Officers Report	30/11/1915	30/11/1915
Heading	5th Division 14th Bde 2nd Inniskilling Fus Went To 96th Bde. 32nd Div. January December 1915		
Heading	Went To 96th Bde. 32nd Div In January. 2nd Inniskilling Fusiliers December 1915		
War Diary	Maricourt	01/12/1915	24/12/1915
War Diary	Sailly Lorette	25/12/1915	31/12/1915
Heading	2 R. Innis Fus 1915 Aug 1915 Oct		

2ND DIVISION
5TH INFY BDE

2ND BATTALION
ROYAL INNISKILLING FUSILIERS
1915 JAN - JUL 1915

5th Inf.Bde.
2nd Div.

Battn. transferred
from G.H.Q. Troops
25.1.15.

WAR DIARY

2nd BATTN. THE ROYAL INNISKILLING FUSILIERS.

JANUARY

1915

2nd Royal Inniskilling Fusiliers.

Army Form C. 2118.

WAR DIARY
or
INTELLIGENCE SUMMARY.
(Erase heading not required.)

Instructions regarding War Diaries and Intelligence
Summaries are contained in F.S. Regs., Part II.
and the Staff Manual respectively. Title pages
will be prepared in manuscript.

Hour, Date, Place		Summary of Events and Information	Remarks and references to Appendices
1915.			
January 1 – 24.	WISQUES	Battalion remained in Reserve.	
" 25th.	WITTES.	Ordered to join 5th Brigade at ROBECQ. Marched to WITTES and billeted.	
" 26th.	ROBECQ.	Marched to ROBECQ and billeted.	
" 28th.	– do –	Battn. inspected by G.O.C. 1st Army and 2nd Division.	
" 29th.	– do –	Attack expected on front line. Battalion ordered up in haste to support, but Germans failed to succeed. Battn. ordered back to billets at ROBECQ.	
" 30th.	LES CHOQUAUX	Marched to LES CHOQUAUX and billeted.	
" 31st.	– do –	Remained in billets at LES CHOQUAUX.	

C A Welchy   Lieut Colonel.
1st Feb. 1915.   Commanding 2nd Royal Inniskilling Fusrs

5th Inf.Bde.
2nd Div.

WAR DIARY

2nd BATTN. THE ROYAL INNISKILLING FUSILIERS.

F E B R U A R Y

1 9 1 5

2nd Royal Inniskilling Fusiliers

WAR DIARY or INTELLIGENCE SUMMARY.
(Erase heading not required.)

Army Form C. 2118.

Instructions regarding War Diaries and Intelligence Summaries are contained in F.S. Regs., Part II. and the Staff Manual respectively. Title pages will be prepared in manuscript.

Hour, Date, Place	Summary of Events and Information	Remarks and references to Appendices
1915. February 1-5. LES CHOQUAUX	Battalion remained in billets at LES CHOQUAUX.	
6th FESTUBERT & LE PLANTIN.	Battalion relieved Oxfords & Bucks L.I. in front trenches. Relief completed at 4 p.m.	
7th. -do-	Work carried on at Breastworks to Hill 10 p.m. Much sniping.	
-do-	Germans heavily bombarded GIVENCHY and shelled our front line without doing damage from 2.30 to 4.30 p.m. Work on breastworks carried on during night.	
8th -do-	Enemy shelled our lines intermittently during the day. Works on breastworks carried on with double digging parties.	
9th -do-	Breastworks occupied by day for the first time. Front line boys occupied breastworks in strength. Reserve boys used every night for continuation of breastworks. Men in actual occupation of breastworks engaged in making shelters and parados.	
10th -do-	At 1 a.m. 2nd Lieut R.J. Woods, who had gone out in search of a supposed spy, was found semi-conscious on road. He reported he had accosted man and ams fired on him, but was in turn knocked down from behind. Work on breastworks and parados continued.	
11th -do-	Work on breastworks continued. One man killed by sniper.	
12th -do-	French attack and demonstrate at 4 p.m. Intermittent shelling of our lines as a result. Work on breastworks carried on. R.A. Telephone wires all cut during the night.	

Army Form C. 2118.

WAR DIARY
or
INTELLIGENCE SUMMARY.
(Erase heading not required.)

Instructions regarding War Diaries and Intelligence Summaries are contained in F.S. Regs., Part II. and the Staff Manual respectively. Title pages will be prepared in manuscript.

Hour, Date, Place	Summary of Events and Information	Remarks and references to Appendices
1915.		
February 13th. FESTUBERT & LE PLANTIN.	Enemy dropped a few shells into our lines. Work on breastworks continued.	
14th. —do—	1600 sandbags filled ready for road barricade. French bombarded Germans at 4 a.m. Battn. relieved by Oxfords and marched to ESSARS and billeted.	
15th – 17th. ESSARS	Remained in billets. Working parties engaged in improving first line entrenchment.	
18th. GORRE	Moved to billets in GORRE	
19th – 21st. —do—	Remained in billets. Working parties engaged in front line.	
22nd. FESTUBERT	Relieved Oxfords in trenches. Foggy night.	
23rd. & LE PLANTIN.	23rd. Three men wounded in front breastworks by enfilade fire from GIVENCHY. Quiet day. No shelling. Completed provisioning of redoubt and thickened breastwork.	
24th. —do—	Work continued on breastworks.	
25th. BETHUNE.	5th. Bde. relieved by 3rd Bde. Battn. relieved by Gloucesters. Marched to billets in BETHUNE.	
26th – 27th. —do—	Remained in billets in BETHUNE.	
28th. CUINCHY.	5th. Bde. relieved 4th. (Guards) Bde. in trenches. Battn. relieved Grenadier Guards in front line trenches.	

C. A. McCemy Lieut. Colonel,
Commanding 2nd R. Inniskilling Fusrs.

5th Inf.Bde.
2nd Div.

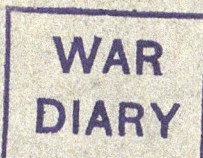

2nd BATTN. THE ROYAL INNISKILLING FUSILIERS.

M A R C H

1 9 1 5

2nd Royal Inniskilling Fusiliers

Army Form C. 2118.

WAR DIARY
INTELLIGENCE SUMMARY.
(Erase heading not required.)

Instructions regarding War Diaries and Intelligence Summaries are contained in F.S. Regs., Part II. and the Staff Manual respectively. Title pages will be prepared in manuscript.

Hour, Date, Place	Summary of Events and Information	Remarks and references to Appendices
1915.		
March 1 - 3. CUINCHY.	Battn. occupied trenches at CUINCHY; the right company being the extreme right of the British line. French troops in occupation on our right.	
4 - 7. BEUVRY.	Billetted in BEUVRY.	
8 - 11. CUINCHY.	In Trenches at CUINCHY. Participated in battle of NEUVE CHAPELLE by covering fire. Casualties – Capt. G.G. Ruett and 2nd Lieut. J.A. Stewart slightly wounded. 5 killed. 21 wounded.	Casualties – 9 men wounded. 5 killed. 21 wounded.
12 - 15. BEUVRY.	Billetted in BEUVRY.	
16 - 19. CUINCHY.	In Trenches at CUINCHY. Casualties 2 killed. 5 wounded.	
20. BEUVRY.	Billetted in BEUVRY.	
21. VENDIN.	Moved to VENDIN LEZ BETHUNE and billetted.	
22 - 24. GORRE.	Moved to GORRE on 22nd, and billetted till 24th.	
25. FESTUBERT.	Relieved OXFORDS in trenches at FESTUBERT. Casualties – 1 killed. 6 wounded.	
29 - 31. – do –	In Trenches at FESTUBERT.	

C A Hickling Lieut. Colonel,
Commanding 2nd Royal Inniskilling Fusiliers.

1st April, 1915.

5th Inf.Bde.
2nd Div.

WAR DIARY

2nd BATTN. THE ROYAL INNISKILLING FUSILIERS.

A P R I L

1 9 1 5

2nd Royal Inniskilling Fusiliers

Army Form C. 2118.

WAR DIARY
or
INTELLIGENCE SUMMARY.

(Erase heading not required.)

Instructions regarding War Diaries and Intelligence Summaries are contained in F. S. Regs., Part II. and the Staff Manual respectively. Title pages will be prepared in manuscript.

Hour, Date, Place	Summary of Events and Information	Remarks and references to Appendices
1915.		
April 1 - 4. FESTUBERT.	In Trenches at FESTUBERT. Casualties :- 1 man killed.	
April 5 - 12. ESSARS.	Billetted in ESSARS.	
" 13 - 18 FESTUBERT.	In Trenches at FESTUBERT. Casualties :- 1 man killed, 4 wounded.	
" 19th — do —	Relieved by 19th London Regiment. Marched to BETHUNE and billetted.	
" 20 - 30 BETHUNE.	Remained in BETHUNE.	

C. A. Wilding
Lieut. Colonel,
Commanding 2nd Royal Inniskilling Fusiliers.
30th April, 1915.

5th Inf.Bde.
2nd Div.

> WAR DIARY

2nd BATTN. THE ROYAL INNISKILLING FUSILIERS.

M A Y

1 9 1 5

2nd Royal • Inniskilling Fusiliers

Army Form C. 2118.

WAR DIARY
or
INTELLIGENCE SUMMARY.
(Erase heading not required.)

Hour, Date, Place	Summary of Events and Information	Remarks and references to Appendices

1915.

May 1 - 3 | Billets MONTMORENCY BKS., BETHUNE.

" 4th, 5th + 6th | Relieved 1st R.R. Regt 6th Infy Bde., in CUINCHY trenches. remained till 6th, Casualties, 4 killed, 6 wounded.

" 7th | Billets BETHUNE.

" 8th | Left billets midnight 8/9 with 5th Bde. and marched to LE HAMEL near GORRE, [where] 5th Bde. remained in support during attack by 1st Division.

" 9th | As above. At 8.30 p.m. Bde. marched to RICHEBOURG ST VAAST, and remained in reserve on road right of 9/10.

" 10th | Battn. moved at 3.30 a.m. to occupy reserve breastworks relieving Oxfords. O.C. Lieut. Col. G.A. Wilding to m.g. hospital, Capt. J.H. Crawford resumed command of Battn. heavy shelling whilst in breastworks. Casualties 4 wounded. At 2 p.m. Battn. was relieved by units of the 6th Bde. and went into billets at RICHEBOURG.

" 11th | Moved to bivouac on LE TOURET road about 4 p.m.

2nd Royal Inniskilling Fusiliers

Army Form C. 2118.

WAR DIARY
or
INTELLIGENCE SUMMARY.
(Erase heading not required.)   2

Hour, Date, Place	Summary of Events and Information	Remarks and references to Appendices
1915.		
May 12th.	8.30 a.m. Moved back to billets in RICHEBOURG. Relieved Oxfords in front breastworks. Two coys in front line and 2 in reserve.	
" 13th.	In breastworks. Casualties 1 killed, 9 wounded.	
" 14th.	As above. Casualties:- 2nd Lieut. W.B.S. Hattocks and J. Blakeney wounded, other ranks 3 killed, 15 wounded.	
" 15th.	As above. Casualties 1 killed, 20 wounded.	
" 15/16th.	At 9 p.m. Battalion formed up in breastworks for attack. "A" & "D" Coys in front line 1st L in support. Attack started at 11.30 p.m. 16th Infy Bde, on our right, and Worcesters on our left.) Right half attack of Battn. was successful, left half failed, also Worcesters and Indian Corps. Remained in captured German trench till evening of 16th, when ordered to withdraw to Reserve breastworks. Casualties:- Killed - Lieut. R.W.B. Hinde, 2nd Lieut. L.M.B. Inordaunt Smith, 2nd Lieut. W.J. Whittington.	

2nd Royal Munsters Fusiliers

WAR DIARY
or
INTELLIGENCE SUMMARY.

Army Form C. 2118.

(Erase heading not required.)

Hour, Date, Place	Summary of Events and Information	Remarks and references to Appendices
1915		
May 15/16th	Casualties continued.	
	Died of Wounds:- 2nd Lieut. J. I. Morgan.	
	Wounded:- Capt. & Adjt. G.R.D. Steward, D.S.O. Captain R.C. Smythe, Capt. C.C. Hewitt, Capt. H.A. Crawford, Lieut. C.A. Daniels (& adjt), Lieut. C.C. Thompson, 2nd Lieuts. J.C. Tudlow, A.C. Lyons, C.C. Moore, C.J. Carter.	
	Wounded and Missing:- 2nd Lieut. J.A. Stewart.	
	Missing (believed killed) Lieut. 18/L.N. Macks, Lieut. C.J.S. Abbott, 2nd Lieuts. H.W. Hyde and A.D. Wingate.	
	Other ranks:- Killed 39; Wounded 341; Missing 239.	
14th	Remained in Reserve breastworks and relieved by 1/1st GURKHAS (SIRHIND Bde) at 12 midnight 17/18th, and marched to billets at LE TOURET.	
18th	The Brigade marched at 3pm. to billets near GONNEHEM.	
20th	The Battalion marched to billets at BURBURE.	
20th - 28th	Battalion remained in billets at BURBURE.	

WAR DIARY

INTELLIGENCE SUMMARY.

(Erase heading not required.) 2nd Royal Inniskilling Fus:rs

Army Form C. 2118.

Instructions regarding War Diaries and Intelligence Summaries are contained in F.S. Regs., Part II. and the Staff Manual respectively. Title pages will be prepared in manuscript.

Hour, Date, Place	Summary of Events and Information	Remarks and references to Appendices
1915.		
May 22nd.	Battn. was inspected by G.O.C. 2nd Division, who expressed his satisfaction at the good work of the Battn. during the action of 15th/16th inst.	
" 24th.	G.O.C. 10th Corps visited Bn. Hd. Qrs. to thank all ranks for their good work during recent operations.	
" 29th.	5th Bde. moved to take over part of line held by 58th French Division. Battalion marched to billets in VERMELLES.	
" 30th. 31st.	Battn. remained in billets at VERMELLES.	

C.A. Vesey
Lieut. Colonel,
Commanding 2nd Royal Inniskilling Fus:rs.
31st May, 1915.

5th Inf.Bde.
2nd Div.

Became I.Corps Troops
21.7.15.

Became Third Army
Troops 25.7.15.

WAR DIARY

2nd BATTN. THE ROYAL INNISKILLING FUSILIERS.

J U L Y

1 9 1 5

2nd Royal Inniskilling Fusiliers.

WAR DIARY
INTELLIGENCE SUMMARY.
(Erase heading not required.)

Army Form C. 2118.

Hour, Date, Place	Summary of Events and Information	Remarks and references to Appendices
1915.		
July 1 – 3	In reserve billets at LE PREOL.	
4 – 8.	In trenches at GIVENCHY. Casualties 1 killed 1 wounded.	
8 – 13.	In reserve billets at LE QUESNOY.	
13.	Moved to Montmorency Bks. BETHUNE.	
19.	Orders received for Battn. to be held in readiness to join 3rd Army	
21.	Moved to billets in Ecole de Jeune Filles, BETHUNE.	
22.	Enemy shelled BETHUNE about 5.30pm. 2 shells landing in billets occupied by Battn. Casualties:- Wounded - Capt. E.A.H. Alexander; Wounded (at duty) Lieut R.B.S. Coar, other ranks - Killed 15, Wounded 59.	
25.	Bn. entrained at Fouquereuil Stn. to join 3rd Army. Proceeded by rail to DOULLENS and marched to billets in TERRAMESNIL.	
25 – 31	Remained in billets at TERRAMESNIL.	

31/7/15.

C.A. Wilding Lieut. Colonel,
Commanding 2nd Royal Inniskilling Fusiliers.

5th Inf.Bde.
2nd Div.

WAR DIARY

2nd BATTN. THE ROYAL INNISKILLING FUSILIERS.

J U N E

1 9 1 5

2nd Royal Inniskilling Fusiliers

Army Form C. 2118.

WAR DIARY or INTELLIGENCE SUMMARY.
(Erase heading not required.)

Instructions regarding War Diaries and Intelligence Summaries are contained in F. S. Regs., Part II. and the Staff Manual respectively. Title pages will be prepared in manuscript.

Hour, Date, Place	Summary of Events and Information	Remarks and references to Appendices
1915. June 1.	Billeted at PHILOSOPHE - VERMELLES.	
2 - 7	Relieved Oxfords in trenches X1 near Fosse No 7 de Béthune on LENS road. Casualties	
7	Batt. relieved by 18th London Regt. 47th Div., and marched to billets at FOUQUEREUIL.	
7 - 15	In billets at FOUQUEREUIL. Coy. Training etc.	
16	Moved to billets at LA BOURSE.	
16 - 19	In billets as Bde. Reserve at LA BOURSE.	
20	Moved to billets in VERMELLES. One Coy. in trenches at LE RUTOIRE as Reserve Coy to Glasgow Highlanders.	
20 - 23	As above. Working parties provided nightly for work on new front line Y1. Casualties 16 men wounded.	
24 - 28	Relieved Oxfords in trenches in Y1. At Ar. Oracat LE RUTOIRE FARM. Casualties 3 men wounded.	

2nd Royal Inniskilling Fusiliers

WAR DIARY
or
INTELLIGENCE SUMMARY.

Army Form C. 2118.

(Erase heading not required.)

Hour, Date, Place	Summary of Events and Information	Remarks and references to Appendices
1915 June 28	Battn. relieved by Gloucester Regt., 3rd Bde., 1st Div. Bn moved to billets in BETHUNE. ECHOLE de JEUNE FILLES arriving 3.30 am. 29th June.	
29	Billets in BETHUNE.	
30th.	Moved to billets in LE PRE OL to relieve 1st Grenadier Guards, 20th Bde.	

C.A. Wilding Lieut Colonel,
Commanding 2nd Royal Inniskilling Fusrs.

3/9/15.

13 H.

3rd Army Troops

12/6598

2nd Royal Inniskillen Fus.d

Vol XIII

From 1 - 31. 8. 15

2nd Royal Inniskilling Fusiliers.

WAR DIARY
or
INTELLIGENCE SUMMARY.
(Erase heading not required.)

Army Form C. 2118.

Hour, Date, Place		Summary of Events and Information	Remarks and references to Appendices
1915. August	1	Bn. furnishes 3 Officers and 140 N.C.Os and men for duty with 3rd Army Troops, and one Officer and 35 men for duty with 4th Corps Hd-Qrs. Lieut Colonel C. A. Wilding D.S.O. took over command of 3rd Army Troops on 26th July 1915. Major J.H. Crawford assumed command of the Battn. from that date.	
"	1	Battalion moved from TERRAMESNIL. 2 Coys. to VAUCHELLES, 2 Coys. and Hd-Qrs. to LOUVENCOURT.	
"	4	Battalion moved to BERTRANCOURT, and took over trenches vacated by 2nd R. Dublin Fusiliers. Battn. attached to 10th Bde. 4th Division, for administration.	
"	4 – 31	Remained at BERTRANCOURT. Battn. engaged in constructing Reserve trenches	
31/8/15.		*J.H. Crawford* Major, Commanding 2nd Royal Inniskilling Fus.	

M

121/6992

14.M.

3rd Army

2nd Royal Inniskilling Fus'rs

Sep 1 15

2nd Royal Inniskilling Fusiliers.

Army Form C. 2118.

WAR DIARY
of
INTELLIGENCE SUMMARY.
(Erase heading not required.)

Instructions regarding War Diaries and Intelligence Summaries are contained in F. S. Regs., Part II. and the Staff Manual respectively. Title pages will be prepared in manuscript.

Hour, Date, Place	Summary of Events and Information	Remarks and references to Appendices
1915. September 1st – 30th. BERTRANCOURT.	Battalion remained at BERTRANCOURT, and was engaged in constructing Reserve Trenches during the month of September, 1915. Four detachments, each consisting of one Officer and 22 other ranks, were furnished by Battalion for road harrying purposes, at ACHEUX, GEZAINCOURT, CORBIE and BERTRANGLES. Detachments at 4th Corps Hd. Qrs. rejoined the Battalion on 23rd Sept. 1915.	

H Maxwell Major.
Commanding 2nd Royal Inniskilling Fusiliers
30th September, 1915.

15.H.

M/21/7429

3rd Army

2nd Quartermaster Gen'l
Vol XV
Oct 15

GHQ

MY
23/11/-

2nd Royal Inniskilling Fusiliers.

WAR DIARY

INTELLIGENCE SUMMARY.

(Erase heading not required.)

Army Form C. 2118.

Hour, Date, Place	Summary of Events and Information	Remarks and references to Appendices
1915. October 1st to 31st. BERTRANCOURT.	Battalion remained at BERTRANCOURT, and was engaged in constructing Reserve Trenches in 4th Corps line. Two companies were ordered to VAUCHELLES on 6th October, for Wood-cutting, under orders of C.R.E. 4th Corps. These companies were relieved by 3rd Entrenching Battalion on 25th October, and returned to BERTRANCOURT.	

J D Dyffen Captain
Commanding 2nd Royal Inniskilling Fusiliers.

1/11/15.

5th Division
14th Bde.
2nd Royal Inniskilling Fus.

November 1915

Came from G.H.Q. Troops
18 Nov. 1915

14th Bde.

5th Div.

Came from G.H.Q. Troops 18th Nov. 1915.

2nd R. INNISKILLING FUSILIERS

NOVEMBER 1915

On His Majesty's Service.

Army Form C. 2118.

WAR DIARY
or
INTELLIGENCE SUMMARY.

(Erase heading not required.)

Instructions regarding War Diaries and Intelligence Summaries are contained in F. S. Regs., Part II. and the Staff Manual respectively. Title pages will be prepared in manuscript.

Hour, Date, Place	Summary of Events and Information	Remarks and references to Appendices
1915.		
November 1st — 15th.	Battalion remained at BERTRANCOURT and was engaged in constructing Reserve trenches in 7th corps line.	
November 16th.	Orders received to move to join 14th Infty Bde, 5th Division.	
November 18th.	Battalion moved by motor buses to BRAY. Detachment from 3rd Army Headquarters rejoined and Battalion marched by coys. to billets at SUZANNE, 2nd line 14th Infty Bde. Lieut. Col. L.O. Wilding, C.M.G. resumed command of the Battalion.	
November 19th.	Remained in billets at SUZANNE. A regrettable accident occurred during the afternoon through some men tampering with an unexploded German shell, found near their billet. The shell exploded, resulting in the death of 3 men and injury to 4 others.	
November 20th.	Battalion relieved 1st D.C.L.I. in trenches in Sub. Sector A.4. Queen Victoria Rifles 15th Bde, on our left and 2nd Battn. Manchester Regt. on our right. "A", "B" and "C" Coys in front line. "D" Coy (in support) and Battn Headquarters in billets	

(9 29 6) W 2794 100,000 5/14 H W V Forms/C. 2118/11

Army Form C. 2118.

WAR DIARY
or
INTELLIGENCE SUMMARY.
(Erase heading not required.)

Instructions regarding War Diaries and Intelligence Summaries are contained in F. S. Regs., Part II. and the Staff Manual respectively. Title pages will be prepared in manuscript.

Hour, Date, Place	Summary of Events and Information	Remarks and references to Appendices
1915		
Nov. 20th (continued).	in MARICOURT village. 2nd Manchesters on our right relieved by 2nd East Surreys on 26th instant.	
Nov. 21st — 30th.	Remained in trenches A4. Each company doing 6 days in front line and 2 in support. Casualties :- O.R. wounded 10.	

C A Wilding Lieut-Colonel,
Commanding 2nd Battalion, Royal Inniskilling Fusiliers.

"C" Form (Original).   Army Form C. 2123 A

MESSAGES AND SIGNALS.

No. of Message..................

Prefix..........Code..........Words..........

	£	s.	d.

Charges to collect

Service Instructions

Received From............... By...............

Sent, or sent out At............... m To...... A 4. By...............

Office Stamp.

Handed in at the............... Office, at............... m. Received here at...... 6.13 ......m

TO 16 Post Rifle

* Sender's Number	Day of Month.	In reply to Number.	AAA

[Handwritten message, partially legible:]

...officer ...report and there was
little ...during ...last night an about
10:30 ...late in the enemy line was
seen ...over their parapet ...
advanced but ...was fired
on and apparently hit and very shortly
after two more Germans crawled over the
parapet and appeared to try and drag
their comrade away and were
fired on but result unknown At
12:30 am the enemy were heard driving in
stakes in front of A.P.L. and about 12 noon
enemy fired five MG rifle shots into SQUARE

FROM	
PLACE	
TIME	

* This line should be erased if not required.

GALE & POLDEN, LTD. PRINTERS, ALDERSHOT.
(69,017). Wt. 7981—443. 40,000 Pads. 4/13. W.

"C" Form (Triplicate).　　　　　　Army Form C. 2123 A.

MESSAGES AND SIGNALS.　　No. of Message..............

| | Charges to Pay £　s.　d. | Office Stamp. |

Service Instructions

Handed in at the................Office, at..............m. Received here at............m.

TO

| Sender's Number | Day of Month. | In reply to Number. | AAA |

aaa for [...] night or nothing
[...] one option German a
machine gun firing very slowly was
heard about midnight in front of
trench 30 aaa transport aaa transport
was heard about 1 am in direction of
MAUREPAS and two pieces of box
pattern were observed in front of
trench 30 aaa their position appeared
prominent and their edge reaches by
6 inches aaa these were only visible
through a telescope aaa

FROM	
PLACE	2nd Innskillings
TIME	5 30 pm

GALE & POLDEN, LTD. PRINTERS, ALDERSHOT.
(69.017). Wt. 7081—443. 40,000 Pads. 4/13. W

Intelligence Officer's Report. to 4 p.m.
2nd R. Inniskilling Fusiliers - 22 Novr 1915.

<u>Sniping</u> - During the day there was very little firing except at A.P.1. Here the Germans shoot at a small tube periscope if it is exposed for long. Their sniping is good and from an oblique direction.

<u>Machine gun</u> - There was no Machine Gun fire during the day. During the night a machine gun fired from the left and right of A P1. It fired at a rate of about 100 rds a minute and its shots traversed AP1 cutting the sandbags of the parapet so that it was dangerous to look out. The men posted in A P1 answered with volleys at the Machine Gun loophole. This appeared successful treatment, as the gun was apparently silenced about 2 a.m. and again about 6 a.m.

<u>Transport</u> - Horse transport was heard in the direction of Hardicourt at 10.30 p.m. In the same direction, motor transport was heard at 12.30 a.m. and a motor cycle at 3. a.m. At 6.15 a.m. horse transport was heard in the direction of the Briquetterie

(2)

<u>German working parties etc.</u> — At 6.50 a.m. a German wearing grey great coat and soft round hat was seen to pass and repass in the German trench in front of A.P₁. He was fired at and did not appear again.

At 7.45 a.m. a German wearing a dark grey tunic and soft hat left the German trench opposite A.P₁ and approached our lines. He was fired at and ~~~~ ran into dead ground.

At 11.30 a.m. the mist lifting a little, about 8 Germans could be dimly seen at work about 200 yards behind the German front line and opposite A.P₁. They were fired at and they were not seen again.

<u>German Flag seen.</u> — About 2 p.m. the fog lifted and a flag was observed about 250 yds in front of SQUARE. It was triangular in shape half red and half dark blue. It was visible for 80 minutes until the fog thickened.

<u>Wind</u> — light N.N.E.

The fog prevented all observation behind the lines and only the trenches on our right front could be seen

for O.C. C.A.M. Alexander Captain
2/R.C. Inniskilling Fus

Intelligence Officers Report to 4 pm
2nd Royal Inniskilling Fusiliers - 23/11/15

Snipers - The German snipers were very active, during the day, in front of AP1. They fire obliquely from loopholes.

German Working Parties etc. - At 12.30 a.m. last night a patrol of 3 Germans were seen to the left of AP1. They were fired on and ran into dead ground. About the same a black dog was seen in front of the German parapet. This was also fired upon and it disappeared.

At 8 a.m. when the mist lifted slightly, about 6 Germans were seen in front of the SQUARE. They were without greatcoats and by their movements appeared to be wiring. They were apparently on the edge of their were nearest to us. They were fired on by our sentries but the fog immediately thickened again.

At 10 a.m. a working party of about 30 Germans was observed straight in front of AP1. They were working apparently about 400 yards behind their front line. They were observed by telescope and it was impossible to be sure of their range. This was in the same locality as the working party seen yesterday, although further back.

(2).

There also appear to be two heaps of timber at this point. It seems likely that during the night and during misty weather work is carried on by the enemy at A11c 25.10.

Wind – Very slight NE.

Uniform etc – Two Germans were observed looking over their parapet in front of T29. They wore dark grey hats with blue bands and apparently a white metal badge.

Forwarded

C.M. Alexander
Capt & OC

Y.R. Innes Lieut

2nd Royal Inniskilling Fusiliers
Intelligence Officers Report 24 Nov 1915.

Sniping - German snipers were fairly active during the night and day.

Machine Guns - There was little Machine Gun fire during the night and none during the day.

Guns - At 6 p.m. 23rd inst. the enemy fired from twenty to thirty shells (small H.E.) from our right front. The shells fell in front of, and in the wire of, T33 and T34, and in left front and in rear of T35. The trenches were undamaged. Our artillery immediately replied.

At 10.30 a.m. ten 77 m.m. HE shells were fired into the rear of the SQUARE and along the east face of BOIS DE MARICOURT. The shells appeared to be fired from A.11.d.30 as smoke was observed which appeared to be the smoke of their discharge.

Three more shells were fired into the same locality about 12.45 p.m.

About twelve more shells were fired behind ORCHARD AVENUE about 3.30 p.m.

These shells all appeared to come from the same guns.

Transport - Horse transport was heard in the direction of Montauban between 7 p.m. and 7.30 p.m.

(2)

moving N. to S. It was again heard about 9.30 p.m.

At 8 p.m. and again at 8.30 p.m. motor transport was heard in the direction of MONTAUBAN.

At 1.15 p.m. a cyclist was observed passing along the GUILLEMONT - MONTAUBAN Road by the edge of the BOIS DE BERNAFAY.

German Working Parties - At 3 p.m. earth was observed being thrown up at A10 c 50 50. Rifle fire was directed on this point and the work apparently ceased.

German Trenches - At A10 d 65 25 there is an outstanding machine gun emplacement with a slot loophole and protected by about 5 feet of heavy timber. This has a projecting piece of light grey coloured iron or zinc piping pointing S.E. This appears to be new and points in the direction of A.P. Two of the enemy were observed this afternoon, talking by the side of the emplacement as though they were on duty there. A.P. has been troubled by a machine gun slowly traversing across its head, and it appears likely that the gun fired from this emplacement.

At about A10 d 75 25 there is what

(3)

appears to be a sheet of iron about 6 feet long by 5 feet wide placed in the enemy front line as though screening a machine gun. These were ~~intended to~~ shown to an artillery officer. ~~~~

General – Trumpet calls were very faintly heard this afternoon and yesterday afternoon about 2.30 p.m. They appeared to be the practising of cavalry trumpeters and to come from the N.W.

At 10.15 a.m. smoke and steam was rising as though from an engine just to the left of MAUREPAS church.

At 3 p.m. a train appeared to be in the HALTE of MAUREPAS.

WIND – Light N.

J.P. Ashire ?/L
3rd Dragoons
attached 2nd R. Iniskilling Dns.

14th Inf Bde

Forwarded.

24/7/15 5-30 p.m.

C.H.W. Alexander
Captain
2/R.E. Inniskilling Dns.

2nd Royal Inniskilling Fusiliers
Intelligence Officer's Report.   25/11/15

Sniping – German snipers were as active as usual during the night and day. Their loopholes are being observed carefully through periscopes and by telescope, and steps are being taken to deal with them.

Machine guns. – There was practically no machine gun fire during the day or night. The new German machine gun reported, has not yet been observed by this regiment.

Artillery – At 2 p.m. one 77 m.m. shell burst in the communication trench immediately behind the SQUARE.

See ✱

✱ About 11.30 a.m. the flash and smoke of a field gun was observed in the belt of 6 trees about 1500x from T 30 in a direction about 40° W of N.

The German construction which has been previously reported and appears like a large dug-out with the door facing S.E. at about A3c 9.0., has been closely observed. Nobody has been seen to enter or leave it, but today at 2.40 pm smoke was seen at its left edge in small puffs at intervals of some 20 secs for two or three minutes.

(2)

This was at the time when an aeroplane was being shelled. It appeared possible that an anti-aircraft gun was being fired from that position.

[See * A sentry reported seeing flashes of gun fire from the same direction during the night. The shell being fired was about an eighteen pounder.]

Aeroplanes -
An enemy aeroplane whose identification marks could be seen, crossed our lines and immediately returned to the German lines at 9.50 a.m. Our guns did not fire at it.

Mine - A mine exploded to our left at considerable distance away at 5.20 a.m. causing a small landslide in THE SQUARE.

Transport - There was considerable transport heard at 10.30 p.m. and 5.30 a.m. on the MONTAUBAN Rd. This appeared to be heavier than the usual horse transport.
The usual horse transport was heard through the night on the HARDECOURT - MAUREPAS Road

Wind - Light to fresh N.W.

(3)

Patrols – No German patrols were seen last night. The black dog previously reported was again seen on the German parapet opposite A.P.2.

JL/Halcrow
2/Lt.
3rd Dorsets
att. 2nR. Innis. Ins.

14th Inf Bde

Forwarded

5-25 pm
25/4/15

E.W. Alexander
Capt & Adjt
2/R.C Innis Fus

2nd Royal Inniskilling Fusiliers

Intelligence Officer's Report - 26 Novr 1915

Enemy's fire - Rifle and machine gun-fire were normal.

Artillery - Ten 77 mm shells burst to the right rear of the SQUARE at 11 a.m. Twelve 77 mm shells burst behind T28 at 3.15 p.m.
A blind shell from right front of T34 fell behind T33 and T34 about 200 yards to their rear at 10.30 a.m.

Trench Mortars - Two trench mortars burst 20x to the right of AP at 2.50 a.m.

Enemy works - A new machine gun emplacement appears to have been made during the night in the German front line at A10 c 0570. It has 3 slot loopholes and appears to be made of sandbags covered with earth and supported by timber.

Aeroplanes - At 10.15 a.m. three enemy aeroplanes crossed our lines from the direction of GILLEMONT and went in the direction of ALBERT. They crossed at intervals of about three minutes. The second was a large 'double-fusilage' plane but two propellers could not be distinguished.

(2).

At 10.30 a.m. two more aeroplanes crossed together from the direction of GILLEMONT to the direction of SUZANNE. They were all fired at by our guns and machine guns.

Bombing - During the carrying out of the Brigade bombing scheme a party of men under Sgt Hollinger went out from T.29. Sgt Hollinger crept to the German wire. He saw a hostile patrol on the other side of the wire and threw his grenades at them. The damage done was unknown.

Artillery Screens - Two German artillery screens are observed. They face about E.N.E. The enemy face of them can just be seen from T.30. They are between enemy first and second line. One, at about A10c3065 is coloured red white and blue thus - → B / W / R

The other at about A10c4065 is coloured red and white thus R ⇌ W.

Enemy cyclist - At 10 a.m. an enemy cyclist was observed passing along GILLEMONT-MONTAUBAN Road into MONTAUBAN.

Wind - Light W.

Note. A full report of the bombing scheme has been sent under separate cover.

J.L. Halcrow 2/Lt
3rd Dorsets att. 2nd R. Innis!

14 Inf Bde
Forwarded 5.5 pm

C.A. Alexander
Capt. a.a.
2/R Inniskns

2nd Royal Inniskilling Fusiliers
Intelligence Officer's Report — 28th Nov 1915

Sniping — During the last 24 hours there was again very much less rifle fire than usual, especially during the night. During the day, although there are not many shots fired, the enemy snipers are alert and it is dangerous to expose oneself. At 4 p.m. a sniper's shield was observed just beside the machine gun emplacement at A.10.d.b.5.25. It was about 12" high and 10" wide with two rings, one on each side, and a small loophole. It was painted grey. A German's head was seen to look over the parapet just before the shot was fired. The rifle was probably fixed, the sniper pulling the trigger when the target was occupied.

New machine gun — The reported new machine gun fired again last night. It was clearly heard to quicken up to about 700 rds per minute. It fired in short bursts. Our centre company again reported that its flashes were seen at our right corner of German Wood. Our right company also reported having seen its flashes from the same direction. The spot was observed by telescope, and a small work which might be a new emplacement is observed just

(2)

to the N.E. of our right corner of German Wood at about A10a 7525.

Artillery Screens - The artillery screens previously reported at A10c 3065 should have been reported as A9b 3055. During the night fresh screens have been added. There are now, in addition to those reported, and in the same locality, one red and white banner facing S.E. thus -

  White ◁▨▷ Red _ about 2' square.

Two similar red and white banners, smaller than the others, about 18" square thus -

  ▨ ▨ - facing N.E

And one yellow banner facing N.E. about 2' square.

Transport - Only very light transport was heard last night.

Aeroplanes - Twenty two of our aeroplanes passed over German lines at 2:30 p.m.

General - This 24 hours was again quiet. Germans were whistling during the night, and smoke from their dugouts could be seen all along the line.

Tot. Holcrow 2Lt.
3rd Dorsets att'd 2nd R. Innis Fus.

2nd Royal Inniskilling Fusiliers
Intelligence Officer's Report - 27th Novr 1915

Enemy's Fire - During the last 24 hours the hostile rifle fire has been much less than usual.
Machine gun fire - the enemy fired only one or two short bursts during the night.
Artillery Fire - About 10.30 a.m. 4 77 mm shells burst round the SQUARE in T28. Two fell about 60x in front of the parapet and the remainder behind the parados. A sentry observing through his periscope reported that he saw the smoke of their discharge at the corner of the wood at A17 B34. The shells certainly came from that direction.

Fourteen more of the same type from the same direction were fired into rear of T28 at 4 p.m. (27th). Two exploding resulted in a communication trench behind T28.

At 5 p.m. 26th instant, twelve small calibre shells were fired at T32 from the direction N.E. They fell in front of our wire and behind our parapet. Three were blind.

Our Fire - Artillery - At cross p.m. 26th inst, 3" Battery of Howitzers fired 10 rounds on German trench opposite A.P., T28. Timber was seen to fly in the air from a direct hit on a dug out.

(2).

New German Machine Gun — The flash of a very rapid machine gun, about 700 rds per minute, which fired two short bursts was located in German Wood.

Enemy Working Party — At 7.20 p.m. a hostile working party in front of T30 was heard from A.P.3 to be driving in stakes for wiring. Volleys of rapid fire were fired in the direction of the sounds. After a short cessation of work they recommenced, but after being again fired at they were not again heard. At 7.45 p.m. a wiring party of ours went out in the same locality and was not fired at.

Enemy Flares — A few enemy white flares sent up in front of T32 appeared to be fired from the support trench, and not from their front trench. The flares were very strong and with a range of about 250 to 300 x.

About p.m. 3 red flares at irregular intervals were sent up to the left of our line.

At 11.30 p.m. there was seen in the same direction a red flare immediately followed by a green flare.

Enemy Work — New work appears to have been done at A10 d 6034. A~~~~~~~~~~~~~~
It appears to be a section of a new support trench.

(3)

Enemy aeroplane — A hostile aeroplane flying fairly low crossed our lines twice at 10.45am. Our guns did not fire at it.

General — There was hardly a shot fired during the night from opposite our right company, where the sniping is usually fairly heavy. A considerable amount of whistling and singing was heard in the German trenches. It is suggested that a relief has taken place.

Wind — None.

J.A. Halcrow 2/L
3rd Dorsets
att'd 2nd R. Innis. Fus.

14. Inf Bde
Forwarded

C.M. Alexander
Captain
2/Rl Inniskilling Fus

2nd Royal Inniskilling Fusiliers
Intelligence Officers Report - 29 Nov'15

Rifle fire - The enemy were again very
quiet during the day and night. They
were however active against Advanced Post
AP7 and fired at it volleys from about
eight rifles at intervals until
midnight. Probably the enemy observed
that fresh wire has been added in
front of this trench and intended
to prevent working parties leaving
the sap.

The snipers shield observed yesterday
is removed today. It is probably a
portable shield.

Machine gun fire - The fast German machine
gun was heard occasionally in very
short bursts during the night and
the day. Its position was not
located.

Coloured Flares - On our left front were
observed at 10 p.m - two green flares
at 10.15 pm - two red flares
at 10.30 pm - two green flares

White flares - these were again clearly observed
to come from some 50x to 100x
behind the German front line.

Light seen - About 7 pm. a beam

(2)

of light like that of a motor head light was seen in the sky above BRIQUETERIE. It was visible for a few seconds only. No motor could be heard. This may have been a searchlight many miles away.

General – Germans were heard during the night whistling opposite A.P. and shouting "Got any Woodbines?"

Wind – Light to fresh. E.S.E.

Mist and heavy rain rendered impossible observation behind the German lines

J.L. Halcrow Lt.
For Lieut Col¹
2nd R. Innis. Fus?

14th Inf Bde.

Forwarded.

24/xi/15

C.H. Alexander
?/?/? Captain

2nd Royal Inniskilling Fusiliers
Intelligence Officer's Report – 30th Nov 1915

Enemy's fire – Rifle fire – There was little rifle fire except during the night. It was chiefly directed against our sap heads.

Machine gun fire – The new fast machine gun opened fire at 7.30 p.m on our sap AP3. It was firing from about A10d33. The artillery were informed and he retaliated with six shrapnel which appeared to burst in the correct spot. Immediately our guns had fired a red flare was sent up from about the position of the machine gun. The machine gun did not fire again during the night.

Artillery fire – There were no shells on our front during this 24 hours.

Transport – At 6.20 p.m. and 10 p.m. light horse transport was heard in the direction of HARDICOURT.

Flares – A Red flare was observed in front of T28 at 10.30 p.m.
At 10.45 p.m a green light (not a flare) was seen for a few seconds at about A11c32.

Searchlight – A searchlight was working during the night a long way to our left front.

(3)

Wind - gentle S.W.

J.H. Haken Lt.
3rd Dorsets
attached
2. R. Innis. Fus.

14th Inf Bde.

Forwarded.

C.M. Alexander
Capt & Adjt.
2/R. Innis. Fus.

[Stamp: 2nd INNISKILLINGS ORDERLY ROOM 30/11/15]

(2)

Germans seen – A German was seen working on top of his parapet at 6:45 a.m. in front of T.28. He was fired at and disappeared.

At 9.15 a.m. three Germans were seen walking along the road running E. & W. S.28.c. They passed in front of MONTAUBAN hedge and entered the village through the orchard. They were walking E. to W.

At 2.30 p.m. a German was seen walking W to E. along the road from BOIS DE BERNAFAY to BOIS DES TRONES. He was dressed in light blue uniform and appeared to be wearing a light blue forage cap – this could not be clearly observed.

At 3.45 p.m. a party of twelve Germans passed along the face of MAUREPAS, going from S to N. They disappeared in the village.

Artillery screens – One of the red and white screens reported yesterday has been removed. Another yellow one has been placed. There are also in addition two small yellow flags close together at about A.10.a.12.

German dug out. At 11 a.m. two Germans with white metal cap badges were seen to enter the large dug out at A.3.c.65.45. They were not observed to leave it.

5th Division
14th Bde.
2nd Inniskilling Fus.
Went to 96th Bde, 32nd Div, January.

December 1915

15th Bde.
5th Div.

17.H.

Went to 96th Bde. 32nd Div in January.

2nd INNISKILLING FUSILIERS

DECEMBER

1 9 1 5

Army Form C. 2118.

2nd Royal Inniskilling Fusiliers.

WAR DIARY
INTELLIGENCE SUMMARY.
(Erase heading not required.)

Instructions regarding War Diaries and Intelligence Summaries are contained in F.S. Regs., Part II. and the Staff Manual respectively. Title pages will be prepared in manuscript.

Hour, Date, Place	Summary of Events and Information	Remarks and references to Appendices
1915.		
December 1 – 8. MARICOURT.	Battalion occupied trenches in Sub-Sector A.4.	
	Weather cold and frosty. Some snow.	
	Relieved in trenches by 2nd Devons on night of 8th and took over MARICOURT DEFENCES.	Casualties. O.R. Wounded Six.
	During tour in trenches, had one Coy. 19th Gloucesters attached to Battn. for instruction in trench duties.	
December 8 – 12.	Battn. in MARICOURT DEFENCES. Furnished mining fatigue of 3 Officers and 321 men daily for work under 184 Coy. R.E.	
12.	Battn. relieved in MARICOURT DEFENCES by 2nd D.C.L.I. and took over trenches in Sub-Sector A.3 from 2nd Manchesters, 9th Royal Scots on our right.	
" 13 – 14	In Sub-Sector A.3. Trenches very wet and muddy.	Casualties – O.R. Killed one. Missing one. Wounded 5.
" 14.	Battn. relieved by 2nd Manchesters, and took over Brigade Reserve billets in SUZANNE.	
" 14 – 15	Right of 14th and 15th in SUZANNE.	

Army Form C. 2118.

WAR DIARY
INTELLIGENCE SUMMARY.
(Erase heading not required.)

Instructions regarding War Diaries and Intelligence
Summaries are contained in F.S. Regs., Part II.
and the Staff Manual respectively. Title pages
will be prepared in manuscript.

Hour, Date, Place		Summary of Events and Information	Remarks and references to Appendices
1915.			
December	16	Battn. relieved 2nd Manchesters in trenches in Sub-Sector A 3. "A" Coy 16th R. Warwicks held centre of our Sub-Sector for instructional purpose.	Casualties O.R. Wounded 2.
"	16-18	In trenches in Sub-Sector A 3.	
"	18	Relieved by 2nd Manchesters and took over Brigade Reserve billets in SUZANNE. Major E.I. MANDERS joined Bn. in relief of Capt. S.B. DUFFIN who proceeded to England.	
"	18-19	nights of 18th and 19th in SUZANNE.	
"	20	Relieved 2nd Manchesters in trenches in Sub-Sector A 3.	
"	20-22	In trenches in Sub-Sector A 3.	Casualties - O.R. Killed one, wounded 4.
"	22	Relieved by 2nd Manchesters in A 3, and took over MARICOURT DEFENCES. Working party of 3 Officers and 324 men found daily for work under 184 Coy, R.E.	
"	22-24	In MARICOURT DEFENCES.	
"	24.	Relieved in MARICOURT DEFENCES by 2nd D.C.L.I. and marched to billets in SAILLY LORETTE. Battn. joined 96th Infy. Bde. 32nd Div.	

Army Form C. 2118.

WAR DIARY
INTELLIGENCE SUMMARY.
(Erase heading not required.)

Hour, Date, Place	Summary of Events and Information	Remarks and references to Appendices
1915.		
December 25. SAILLY LORETTE.	Christmas Day. Church Parade in billets. Reinforcements – 55 other ranks arrived.	
December 26-29	In billets at SAILLY LORETTE.	
" 30.	Battalion moved to billets. Hd. Qrs. and 2 Coys to MILLENCOURT and 2 Coys to LAVIEVILLE.	
" 31.	In billets as above. Orders received that Battn. would go into trenches near AUTHUILLE on 2nd January, 1916, with 96th Infy. Bde. Battn. ordered to be held in readiness to join 36th (Ulster) Division between 6th and 8th January, 1916.	
1.1.16.	Commanding 2nd Royal Inniskilling Fusiliers. C.A.Wilderf Lieut. Colonel.	

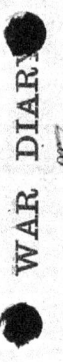

32 DIV

96 Bde

2 R. Innis Fus

1915 Aug   1915 Oct

Box 2179

www.ingramcontent.com/pod-product-compliance
Lightning Source LLC
Chambersburg PA
CBHW081451160426
43193CB00013B/2441